CHRISSY BRENT

THE HAPPINESS ADVANTAGE

The Essential Guide on How to Achieve
Overflowing Happiness, Discover Ways on How To
Cherish Your Life and Be Joyful All the Time

Descrierea CIP a Bibliotecii Naţionale a României
CHRISSY BRENT
    THE HAPPINESS ADVANTAGE. The Essential Guide on How to Achieve Overflowing Happiness, Discover Ways on How To Cherish Your Life and Be Joyfull All the Time / Chrissy Brent. – Bucharest: Editura My Ebook, 2020
    ISBN

CHRISSY BRENT

THE HAPPINESS ADVANTAGE

The Essential Guide on How to Achieve Overflowing Happiness, Discover Ways on How To Cherish Your Life and Be Joyful All the Time

My Ebook Publishing House
Bucharest, 2020

"Remember happiness doesn't depend upon who you are or what you have; it depends solely on what you think."

~Dale Carnegie~

TABLE OF CONTENTS

CHAPTER 1

THE HAPPINESS GENES

Image: FreeDigitalPhotos.net

Happiness is a highly wanted state for most people but it remains to be a lifelong quest for everyone. No one can just claim happiness for one moment, sit back, and watch it linger and stay. It does not discriminate too.

Happiness is often associated with big smiles and boisterous laughter. There is more to happiness than those two. You will discover as you go along the book that happiness is not only defined by happy moments in one's life. If this were the case, then no one would ever have the right to claim happiness.

There are traits that happy people share, regardless of what personality they have. However, happiness is not limited to one type of personality. An outgoing, friendly person is not happier than a shy, reserved person simply because the former is more expressive of whatever happiness he or she has.

Higher Self-worth

The most visible trait of happy people is an adequate sense of self-worth. They know that they have imperfections but they also recognize their beauty and strengths. Moreover, they do not let their weaknesses rule over their lives. Feelings of insecurity may threaten to harm one's self-image once in a while but it does not have to destroy the entire state of happiness. Happy people know how to deal with and overcome their insecurities. They recognize their weaknesses but they never dwell in fault-finding. Fault-finding is very damaging to one's emotional health and well-being. Rather, happy people see their weaknesses as an opportunity to improve.

Sharing Low Moments

Happy people also have their share of low moments in life. They do not have it easy all the time. What sets them apart from miserable people is their positivity. Positivity is not a blind sense of optimism. To have a blind sense of optimism is to set expectations to high that they do not synchronize with reality anymore. Even in the face of despair, happy people still find the strength to remain positive. Although positivity will not give them definite and instant solutions to their problems, they know that doses of positivity will give them the energy and strength to weather any kind of problem. It is all about the mindset.

Contentment

Happy people know the meaning of contentment and know how to live by it. They know that they cannot have everything they want whenever they want it but it does not mean that it should be a reason to mope around and be miserable. Even if obstacles come their way, happy people know how to acknowledge their blessings and be thankful for them. Contentment is being satisfied with whatever one has. However, it should not be confused with complacency. A person can still be content even in pursuit of an ambition. The important thing is not to take the existing blessings for granted.

Because a happy person is the epitome of contentment, he or she should be able to know how to show appreciation and gratitude to the people around. Happiness is a state worthy of celebration, which should be manifested by appreciation and gratitude. It goes beyond saying "thank you" to the people who make one happy, although expressing gratitude towards other people plays a big role in happiness. It is tied with contentment and positivity.

Even if there are bleak moments in life, it should not stop a person from expressing gratitude for the smallest blessings.

Laughter Is The Best Medicine

Laughter is always linked to happy people. Happy people have a sense of humor and know when to have a good laugh, even when they are facing a huge problem. It is not only the comedians that have a wicked sense of humor. One need not laugh only at things that are intentionally funny.

Happy people know how to laugh at themselves once in a while. They do not take life too seriously because embarrassing things happen every now and then. Dealing with problems is a lot easier with a little sense of humor.

Pursue Of Passion

Happy people know that there is an active dimension in happiness. It is not merely a concept or a state. They live and exemplify happiness by doing what they love and what puts a smile on their faces. A happy person pursues passions relentlessly. They cultivate their talents and develop their interests. The joy that they get in pursuing their passions is what gives them fuel to live life to the fullest and attain happiness. Happy individuals do not waste time in doing things that bore them and stunt their growth and self-fulfillment. They heed the call of their passions in order to become the best individuals that they can be. They get happiness in pursuing their passions because it enables them to be the best in their field.

Be Assertive

A sign of happiness is assertiveness too. Assertive is not always linked with aggression. When a person is assertive, it does not necessarily mean that he or she will employ intimidation and violence to get the job done. Rather, an assertive person will make sure that his or her thoughts are expressed clearly. A person can be assertive while still being sensitive to other people's feelings and needs. Assertiveness is important in happiness because some circumstances will push the person to the ground. Assertiveness will let oneself and the whole world know that he or she is not happy with something. Assertiveness is doing something about things that need to be changed.

Spread Happiness

Happiness is infectious. Happy people know how to spread the happiness they feel to the people they interact with, whether through a one-time encounter or regular basis. There are even studies that show that happy people tend to have more stable and strong relationships. Genuinely happy people treat others with kindness, respect, and sincerity – just the way they want to be treated. Happy individuals find it easy to connect with other people because they are able to look past the flaws and imperfections of others. Positivity should be exercised not only in situations concerning the self. Life is a lot easier when you focus on the good traits of other people too. It will be easier for people to be kinder to you if they see that you are willing to focus on their good side. A healthy social interaction with people is undeniably crucial to happiness.

Forgiving

Mistakes are inevitable, even in human relationships. Even happy people are vulnerable to hurt and pain inflicted by their loved ones. Nobody is perfect. Happy people know this but they do not let it ruin their lives. As hard as it may seem, happy people know how to practice the art of forgiveness. When they get hurt, they allow themselves an ample amount of time to heal and lick their own wounds. But after that, they start opening themselves to the possibility of forgiving those that have hurt them. Happy people know that when they are finally ready to forgive, they will set themselves and the people that have hurt them free from anguish and guilt.

As you can see, traits (and not personality types) are listed above. Both shy and outgoing people can have a good sense of humor. Conservative and liberal-minded people can share the same kind of optimism, even if they have opposing views on different issues. Happiness is not exclusive to one personality. It can be achieved by anyone that can exemplify the minimum traits listed above.

CHAPTER 2

THE CAUSE OF UNHAPPINESS

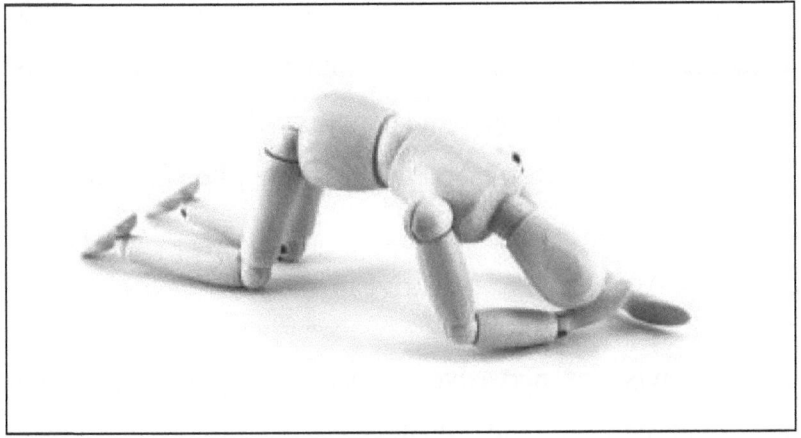

Image: FreeDigitalPhotos.net

Happiness can be elusive for most people. It is rare to find a person that will claim to have attained real happiness. Maybe at some point, they may have declared that they have already attained real happiness but they retract their declaration when disheartening obstacles come along.

Happiness is not determined by what happens to a person. Happiness is a product of how a person reacts to the events that happen in life. Happiness is attained when a person steers life towards its direction. There is no single map for happiness that everyone should follow. It is a path discovered through individual experience.

Even though each one has a different path cut out for happiness, there are a few common causes that cause unhappiness. People's individual reasons for unhappiness are personal but they share general themes more often than not.

Negativism

Negativism is pervasive in many unhappy people. Both happy and unhappy individuals have had to weather many storms in life but it is their mindset that sets them apart. Happiness is drawn from positivity in the faces of adversity. It is positivity that keeps them going and gets them to a sound solution. Negative people think of the worst and as a result, the worst usually happens. Even though the proper mindset will not get a person the exact desired result, it motivates the person to

18

get past challenges and obstacles. Negative thoughts are created out of habit but they eventually become a long-term mindset if the person does not keep tabs of it. When a person gets used to thinking negatively, it becomes hard to get rid of such thoughts. Unhappiness is hard to attain because of destructive, negative thoughts that are difficult to eliminate because they have become ingrained already.

Unhappiness is also caused by the negativity expressed towards other people. It is hard to get along with other people when the worst is assumed of them. It is normal for a person to be defensive and realistic when dealing with people but when it gets out of hand, the negativity becomes hurtful and offensive. It pays to give people the benefit of the doubt. There are a handful of unhappy people that easily judge and mistreat others. This negativity, although expressed towards other people, can rub on oneself. It is very important to be aware of how negativity creeps into one's system because it becomes the root of all other terrible things that lead to unhappiness.

Greediness

Greediness brings people several steps closer to unhappiness. It should not be confused with ambitiousness. A healthy amount of ambitiousness should be good for a person because it motivates a person to improve and progress. Greed, on the other hand, is an extreme thirst for things in life to the point of obtaining it in unjust and unethical ways. Greed is a primary cause of suffering and unhappiness in many people. People become greedy because of the blinding charm of possessions and power. Greed motivates them to seek more things that they need just so the people around them will not have as much they have. These things bring one euphoric pleasure but not long-term happiness. Insatiable greed causes a person to confuse pleasure with happiness. People pursue pleasure hoping to find permanent happiness only to go on an empty search with no end. This constant search for pleasure generates more greed, until such time that the unhappiness and discontent of a person becomes so difficult to contain already. Greedy people refuse to accept the fact that they cannot have everything that they want in life in one pursued.

Envy and jealousy

Greed is related to envy and jealousy. Envy and jealousy are the green monsters that are catalysts to greed. When a person is envious of another person's achievements and belongings, he or she wants to get ahead of that person. Envy will consume the person so much that it can even develop hatred for the object of envy. Soon, the person will derive pleasure in seeing a person suffer. Envious and jealous people also feel terrible when others gain in life. That's why they have the urge to pull people down so that they can feel better about themselves. Envy and jealousy are undeniably negatives states. For many people, they can only go away when a person is happy. However, envy and jealousy are hindrances to happiness themselves.

Envy and jealousy occur when one starts comparing himself and what he has with others. A healthy competition never really hurt anyone. However, getting overzealous with competition may spark envy. Envy and jealousy have already brought down nations, sparked wars, hurt friendships, and destroyed relationships. Envy, without a doubt, can cause a great deal of misery and unhappiness in any community.

Pride

Pride also causes a lot of problems with happiness. The danger of pride stems from the fact that it hinders people in doing the right thing, even if they are completely aware that they are doing the wrong thing. They refuse to budge and change what they have to change simply because they do not want to be proven wrong. People with a false sense of pride cannot be proven wrong, causing them to justify their wrong actions. Pride is also a characteristic of highly insecure people. Proud people are unhappy people because they cannot handle criticism well. They need a constant stream of praises to keep their self-esteem in check. Pride is a blindfold that covers one's vision from reality. It provides temporary relief (particularly if someone feeds that pride) but it only create a false sense of happiness. In the long run, proud people cannot be happy because they are not at peace with themselves. It is also difficult for proud people to attain happiness under any situation their pride makes them inflexible and unable to adapt to various things life throws at them.

Anger

It is natural for a person to feel angry when agitated or hurt. It is part of every being's nature. It is but a defensive mechanism for every animal to protect themselves. A bitch will naturally get angry and fight any being that threatens to harm or take away her puppies. However, lingering anger does not count as a protective defense mechanism because it hinders the person from attaining real happiness. Anger has to be managed well so that it does not escalate to something worse, like hatred. It is almost impossible to stop anger, since it is a natural response of any animal. However, changing the mindset will help control anger.

As mentioned earlier, happiness is a response to certain situations. Anger is a reaction to certain situations as well. By changing the mindset, you can minimize the anger that you feel. For instance, you get really annoyed whenever the colleague you closely work with is always late. It really gets to your nerves because his tardiness is already affecting your overall productivity. He has not changed even after you have already talked to him about this. You can change your mindset instead and still retain your productivity. While waiting for him, you can accomplish other tasks that do not require his efforts. When he arrives, you have fewer tasks to finish. That way, you can channel your anger to something else. Anger can be sparked by petty things but these little things can build up and cloud your perspective. Awareness to situations that cause anger is a key to controlling the raging emotion.

Guilt

When you feel like you have done something wrong, chances are you will be bothered by it unless you do something to make it right. The same feeling goes for someone that thinks that he or she should have done something more than what has been done. It is difficult to attain happiness with guilt being an impediment. Guilt can really be an obstacle in the journey to happiness. It holds down a person, much like quicksand. Guilt can cause internal turmoil that will disrupt peace of mind. No one can be truly happy without being at peace with oneself. The best way to deal with guilt is to address the specific cause. If you have sinned against anyone, muster the courage to apologize to that person. Face the consequences of any of your wrongdoings. Stop running away from problems because this will only heighten any guilt that you feel. The solution to guilt is really simple – face the real reason. It is gathering enough courage that is difficult but once you get past this, you will feel a lot better.

Stress

Finally, stress can become a real barrier in achieving happiness. Activities, hobbies, relationships, and work keep a human being's life meaningful and productive. But sometimes, people do not know when to take it easy.

Having too many activities and priorities will make you forget the purpose of them all. You will fail to enjoy the fruits of your labor, letting you lead a directionless life. The sad thing about it is that you waste energy on something with no purpose. Stress also brings down one's resistance and energy, increasing the vulnerability to negative emotions (i.e. anger). That is why it pays to organize one's life and set priorities straight.

In this day and age, multi-tasking is essential. Many people will make your believe that you will get more done if you do more things at the same time. But there are also dangers in multi-tasking. It is one of the top reasons that stress people out. Moreover, it prevents the person from relishing the essence of what he or she is doing. People focus too much on finishing as many things as possible that they forget to do things properly. This leads to inefficiency and stress. People should learn to separate busyness from stress. Happy people need to be busy with something but if they over do it, they will burn themselves out with stress.

Negativity, greed, pride, envy, anger, guilt, and stress are the most common general reasons that lead to unhappiness. People have individual and personal reasons that are stopping them from achieving happiness but more often than not, they can be traced to the reasons listed above.

CHAPTER 3

LIVING A LIFE FULL OF HAPPINESS

Image: FreeDigitalPhotos.net

Goals in life change from time to time. As soon as one goal is achieved, a person usually moves on to the next one. But there is one common goal that binds humanity – happiness. No one can ever dictate what makes a person happy but there are certain guidelines that one can follow to reach personal happiness. These general guidelines are meant to be flexible. They should be tweaked according to one's lifestyle, goals, and principles. You will find that a happy life is not a privilege. It is something that you work for.

Happiness is a both a choice and a responsibility.

Taking Care of the Body

Although happiness does not rest on the physical body, one's lifestyle is affected by health and (to a certain degree) physical appearance. As they say, you feel good when you look good. Also, you will have more determination and zest for life if your body is in good shape. You need physical energy to work for your happiness. Your physical energy will affect your emotional, spiritual, and mental energy. Your physical health also affects your mood, which is a building block of happiness.

The rules for good health are simple yet difficult to follow for most people – right diet, regular exercise, enough sleep, regulated stress levels, avoidance of vices, etc. It is not just about the maintenance of weight. Nowadays, taking care of the health seems to be equated with losing weight and keeping the body slender and trim. A person needs to take care of the health to ensure that all the faculties in the body are functioning well enough for daily activities. There have been studies conducted on the clinically depressed, showing how regular exercise significantly improved their mood and disposition. A person is more likely to feel a sense of self- worth with good health.

Rely on a Solid Support Group

It is part of human nature to be a social being. There have been studies showing that mortality rates are doubled for people who spend most of their lives in loneliness. Life's problems are easier to deal with when you have a supportive set of family and friends so that you have someone you can share experiences with. Even people that constantly keep to themselves seek the company of their family and/or circle of friends. Every human being needs to feel that he or she is connected with someone. Everyone needs to feel like they are a part of something.

To be happy, a person can't just surround himself or herself with any group of people. The people you are with will have a big impact on your disposition. If you stay with people that are constantly bitter, chances are their bitterness will rub off on you. The same principle applies if you are surrounded by a cheerful and optimistic bunch. Even if you have a mind of your own, you can still imbibe the habits of other people. Keep your distance from negative-minded people and emotional vampires. Seek the support of happy and optimistic people. Let happy people influence your life.

Make an effort to spend time with those you love and nurture existing relationships. There are so many things that you can do, from a phone call to a short visit to a conversation over a few bottles of beer. You should also build new, quality relationships if you can.

Set Goals and Pursue Your Passions

Spontaneity adds zest to life but too much of it will lead a person astray. Having a direction in life is essential to one's happiness. Man needs to be guided by certainty up to a particular degree. Everyone needs some kind of direction. The sense of accomplishment one experiences when a goal is reached is exhilarating. Human beings thrive in challenges and will always aim for something new and stimulating.

Achievements are also a healthy booster for the ego. Any attained goal will make a person happy. It will keep him or her inspired.

You should set aside some time to ponder on your long-term goals in life. You should ensure that you want your goals enough to stick to them even you stumble upon trials along the way. At the same time, you should leave enough room for changes and flexibility. After all, you will never know what will happen along the way. Once you have made your long-term goals, probe deeper into them and extract short-term goals out of them. What can you accomplish in a shorter period of time from a long-term goal? Dividing your goal into manageable pieces will keep your motivated in achieving your goals.

Never set your goals haphazardly. If your heart is not into it, then do not make something your goal. You should live your life fulfilling your dreams and pursuing your passions. If you have a passion for something, embrace it. Pursue it relentlessly but smartly. If you love it enough, you will set aside time for a carefully-crafted plan. It is only by living out your passions will you ever get the endless energy needed to be happy.

Always have a Reality Check

"Reality check" may already have a negative connotation because it is associated with the harsh truth. However, no one can be happy in this world if the happiness that one perceives only exists in a world that does not even exist. It is perfectly fine to ask work for something that you do not have but do not detach yourself from this world completely. In creating a goal or pursuing a path, you should always remind yourself to make your moves attainable. Disappointment comes from unmet expectations.

No one should settle for anything less. However, no one will ever get anywhere if they reach too high for the sky but do not keep their feet firmly planted on the ground.

Random Acts of Kindness

A little kindness never hurt anyone. As a matter of fact, a little kindness will take you a long way when it comes to happiness. It was mentioned earlier that human beings cannot live by their lonesome forever. In relation to that, kindness in human relations is essential to attaining happiness. You should not be blindly kind to anyone by giving away your trust with abandon. Not everyone in this world is to be trusted right away. However, give kindness that is due to each person that you encounter. Did your husband have a long day at work? Offer to take his turn with the chores. Is your mother having a difficult time coping with menopause? Talk to her calmly, even if she snaps at you for no reason at all. Have you noticed that your colleague has been spending extra hours in the office? Offer to help him or her in any way you can. Even acts as simple as opening doors or letting the old lady have your seat in the train will help in making you happy. When you make people smile, you make yourself smile too.

Stay Positive

You have heard this many times but you should know by now that this is easier said than done. Nonetheless, it should not stop you from staying positive. Happy people do not wait for optimism to come into their lives because create opportunities of optimism for themselves. No matter how many unfortunate events plague them, they still find a way to let optimism rule the situation. People who stay positive know how to look for opportunities in trying times. It is not easy to become an optimistic person when you hit the ground really hard. It takes courage to find opportunities to grow in times of trial but people that are able to do so learn new lessons and emerge as stronger individuals.

Being optimistic does not mean that you should turn a blind eye on reality. Optimistic people still keep their feet firmly planted on the ground. They know that bad things can turn up unexpectedly but nonetheless, they still believe that they can do something about it. Genuinely happy people know that happiness is not determined by the events that happen in his life.

Rather, it depends on how they react to it. When negative thoughts start rushing through your head, replace them with more positive and pro-active thoughts.

Avoid Comparison With Others

Your happiness is in danger the moment you start comparing yourself to other people. Comparing yourself to other people will spark envy and jealousy, two of the most prominent causes of unhappiness. Your happiness is your own responsibility and other people's happiness is theirs. Everyone has different experiences so there is really no point of comparing. You can only relate your experiences with others and perhaps, learn from them. But social comparison will lead you nowhere. When you compare yourself to others, you ignore all the progress that you have made with yourself.

Comparing yourself with other people does not make you a happier person. It will only generate bitterness. Everyone deserves to be happy, including you. The only person you should compare yourself with is your older version. Strive to become a better person every day. As for other people, be happy for them. Do not compare yourself to them. If you see admirable traits and achievements in a person, let them serve as your inspiration.

Never Keep Grudges

Hurt and pain are a natural part of human existence. You cannot control the bad things that are happening around you. You can only do so much to avoid getting hurt but there will be no assurance that you will be immune to it. When you get hurt, you should give yourself time to lick your wounds and comfort yourself. However, you should not let the hurt linger longer than it should. You may have been hurt by a family member, friend, or someone else you know. It comes to a certain point when you should stop hurting for your own benefit. You will put yourself in danger when you stay angry, bitter, and hurt for too long. Let go of your grudges to save on emotional space. Save that emotional space for happiness.

Count Your Blessings and Show Gratitude

Humans always seek more than what they have. They love the feeling of accomplishing something, obtaining new things, and enjoying more blessings. In the quest for such, they tend to take things for granted and forget that they already have existing blessings. They get so caught up with their huge ambitions that they forget their small accomplishments. The big things can bring in great joys but the little things also make a big difference in your life. Savor the little accomplishments and show gratitude for the blessings that you encounter on a daily basis. A lot of happiness can be found in the little blessings too. Take your time to enjoy them.

Keep a Wicked Sense of Humor
and Learn How to Relax

Life without laughter is an unimaginable life. Life is meant to be lived to the fullest but it should not be taken too seriously. You can never control certain events so you need to learn to laugh, even when something embarrassing or humiliating happens.

There are scientific studies that prove that laughter significantly benefits the health. It brings down blood pressure and stress hormones. It also boosts the immune system and triggers the release of endorphins, otherwise known as the "happy hormones". Laughter gives the person an improved sense of well-being because by learning how to laugh in problematic times, the person learns how to view the problem in a new and lighter perspective. When you laugh at a problem, you are reassuring yourself that you can handle it. Laughter reinforces optimism and positive thoughts within you.

People ought to learn how to relax nowadays. The world is getting busier by the minute and relaxation is now becoming a luxury. There should be a time for everything, including relaxation. Your senses have to be recharged once in a while. Besides, stressed people find it really hard to be unhappy.

The following listed above are just guidelines. It is highly encouraged that you follow them but you should modify them according to your lifestyle as well.

CHAPTER 4

HAPPINESS IN DIFFICULT TIMES

Image: FreeDigitalPhotos.net

A very common obstacle to real happiness is the mindset that happiness can only truly be attained when one has reached a stage of life that is devoid of problems. If you see life in this perspective, it will be absolutely impossible to gain happiness in this lifetime. Challenges and problems will never cease to come until the day you die. It is but part of every human existence. It is futile to run away from problems because they will only get bigger if you avoid them.

Challenges can give great discomfort and can set you back by a few steps in any of your goals. But no one in this world has ever gone through life without getting tangled up with problems. Nobody can ever deny their existence and you can only do so much to prevent their occurrence. There is really no point in living a life running away from problems. You will encounter all sorts in your lifetime – finance, work, death, relationships, health, etc. But whatever problem you have in your hands, you need to tweak your perception of your problems.

Any challenge can be seen as an obstacle that will prevent you from moving forward or you can think of it as a ledge or stepping stone to push you to the top. Perception matters a lot in how you face problems and handle compromising situations in life. If you think that a problem is a mere obstacle, it can stunt a person's development and growth. If a challenged is perceived as an opportunity to learn, then it can facilitate and bolster growth. For example, Sally's savings has depleted because of unexpected health costs because of her husband's mild stroke attack. Her husband was able to recover with religious therapy sessions but it was her bank account that took the fall. Since her husband had to quit work, she was the sole breadwinner of their family of 4. Yet, she did not see her misfortune as a reason to sulk and wallow in depression. She had finances to fix and a family to feed. She moved her entire family to a smaller apartment and sold their house. She rented an apartment near her office and moved her school- age kids to a school nearby to save on transportation costs. The entire family cut down on their weekend getaways. Sally thought of selling their car but she thought of putting it up for occasional rental services for short-term tourists instead. She tapped into her all her contacts and relied on referrals to ensure that her clients were trustworthy. She priced her rentals at a slightly lower rate than most rental services but her profits were enough to pay off some of her bills. When she was finally able to pay off her medical bill debts, she started investing in a low-scale franchise to keep the cash flow constant. Sally refused to believe that her husband's sickness would ruin her finances and her family's stability. On the contrary, she was able to pull her family out of that financial rut. Moreover, it taught her that she should not just rely on her job for financial security. She should also make investments.

Challenges and problems are often associated with change. It is difficult to deal with change, especially when you have grown comfortable with something or someone. There are some changes that are difficult to deal with, such as changes concerning relationships and career. Jake was happy with his job as a sales executive in a medium-scale company. He was earning a decent sum of money and his supervisor was very considerate and nice. He has also formed friendships with several officemates of his.

However, things took a turn when his girlfriend of five years got pregnant. He was happy with his income but he needed a higher paying job in order to support their child. Coincidentally, another company contacted him and offered him a higher position with higher pay. Jake knew that it was good for his family and the growth of his career, although he was afraid to transfer to a new company because it was a little farther from his apartment. Plus, he did not want to have to adjust to a new set of co-workers. However, his co-workers helped him realize that he needed to embrace this change in order for him to provide a better life for his family. The challenge of adjusting to a new company would also be worth the effort because it would improve his career standing.

A challenge can be conquered easily if the changes that come with it are readily welcomed. Challenges will introduce you to changes that can be very daunting. However, adapting to the changes will enable you to overcome challenges. These changes will make you a better person and teach you more lessons that will bring you closer to happiness.

The problem with running away from challenges is that you will never know how it is supposed to benefit you. It takes a critical mind to see that challenges are more than just a big pain in the ass. You have to understand what the challenge is trying to teach you and what you can get out of it. If you believe that the challenge will make your life better, only then can a challenge bring you true happiness.

Brandon and Leslie have already been together for five years. They were already thinking about tying the knot so they started talking about their options. The couple talked about their future home, the number of kids they were planning to have, and how they would allocate their budget for the house. Leslie's job required her to be based in a foreign country every six months. Brandon, however, already had his own business that gave him enough control of his time. Brandon wanted to have children right after marriage but Leslie wanted to stay in her company for a few more years to build her network and gain more experience. Brandon already wanted to start a family. His mind was telling him to end their relationship, since Leslie clearly did not want the same thing that he wanted that moment.

However, he could not see himself being with anyone other than Leslie. Both of them thought their options through and decided to postpone the wedding for another two years. This would give Leslie enough time to travel and gain more work experience so that she can get a higher position that would not require her to travel as much. Although Brandon was already bent on having children, he opted to look at other options and use the waiting time to expand his business and secure his future with Leslie and their family.

He was able to upgrade his business just in time for their wedding. In addition to that, they were able to buy a 4-bedroom house with ample space for their future children's playground. Had they not saved up for two more years, they would not have been able to buy the house. Most of all, they were able to prove to each other their love and loyalty because of their willingness to wait for the right time.

Handling a challenge properly requires an open and critical mind. Looking at the gifts that the challenges have to offer will bring you closer to happiness.

Any challenge that comes your way is yours. If there is anything that blocks your way, it is your right to take away whatever barricade is causing you trouble. Hiro's mother died in an unfortunate car crash. Being new to the country, he was left with no one else but his father and younger brother.

Back when his mother was alive, she and her father both had separate income. Their combined income was enough to send him and his younger brother to school. However, with his mother gone, his father could only afford to send one child to school. Hiro let his brother take the opportunity but he refused to put education at the bottom of his list. Hiro applied for a working student scholarship. He worked in school as a research assistant. During his spare time, he would edit videos so that he could have money to spare for miscellaneous expenses.

It was not Hiro's fault that his mother died. However, he had to do something about his studies because no one else would. He badly wanted to study so he accepted the challenged and acknowledged the fact that he was an empowered individual with a responsibility to nurture his own self- growth. Be responsible for your own challenges.

If you encounter an obstacle while fulfilling a goal, remember why you are aiming for the goal in the first place. Always remind yourself why you took on the goal in the first place. This is what trainers always tell their athletes when they face a slump during their training. At the beginning of the training, the athletes are all psyched up to wake up early in the morning for a 4-hour training session. They eventually get tired of the routine and the rigors of athletic training. When this happens, they are always reminded of the competition or tournament they are training for to get them back on track.

No one is vulnerable to challenges and obstacles in this earthly life. They make life very dynamic and if perceived in the right way, give the person a more meaningful existence. Most of all, conquered challenges will bring the person to real happiness. The person will linger in happiness knowing that he or she has enough capacity to grow, learn, and conquer all the challenges and trials.

CHAPTER 5

ACHIEVING HAPPINESS IN RELATIONSHIPS

Image: FreeDigitalPhotos.net

Why Relationships Are Important in Attaining Happiness

Relationships - whether romantic, familial, or friendly - cannot be taken out of the happiness equation. Many of the qualities of a person are developed in interactions and relationships. A person needs to belong to an institution built by people to survive. People need to be connected to others in order to find more fulfillment in their development as individuals. People become better versions of themselves with the help of other people.

Even scientific studies can back up the importance of relationships in a one's development and well-being. Humans need to be able to relate to others as early as their infancy stage. Social interaction and well-established relationships are crucial in all areas of a child's development – emotional, intellectual, social, etc. Children who feel more secure and at ease with the relationships they have established are quicker to develop because they can explore their environment, knowing that they can rely on someone for guidance and support. Children perform better in academic and extra-curricular activities when they are well-connected with their teachers, peers, and parents.

There are also studies that show that the happiest people are those that are engaged in close relationships with their spouse, family, and friends. They feel a great sense of belonging, which is really important in happiness.

People with good relationships also live healthier, happier, and longer lives.

One cannot talk about happiness without including relationships. Wherever you may be and whatever you may become, the importance of good relationships cannot be emphasized well-enough. Since human beings are social creatures, it is almost automatic that they will engage in relationships and social interactions. However, building good relationships takes conscious effort. It is not only the presence of relationships that will determine your well-being; strained relationships do not contribute to happiness.

In order to achieve genuine happiness, you must engage in genuine relationships as well. You have to nurture your relationships with your partner, spouse, parents, children, relatives, friends, co-workers, and even acquaintances.

Expectations

Not many people realize that many relationships fail because of unmet expectations. Expectations are normally associated with romantic relationships but they are also prevalent in other relationships. No one can completely do away with relationships. When you establish a close relationship with someone, you are obliged to do certain things for and with that person. For instance, a mentor is expected to provide guidance to a student. An elder brother is usually tasked to look out for his younger siblings. Expectations are not a completely bad thing because it partly gives definition to a relationship.

Expectations in a relationship become toxic when they are set too high. In a romantic relationship, there are certain expectations that should come naturally. You should expect love, affection, companionship, and support.

However, there are some couples with unrealistic expectations for each other. There are girlfriends or wives that expect their husbands to drive for them wherever they go. Some boyfriends and husbands expect their partners to take care of them the way their mothers do. While it is not bad for partners to oblige to personal expectations, it shouldn't be taken against another party if some expectations are not met. In the first place, the involved parties should be clear with each other on expectations.

Unrealistic expectations are also visible in other relationships. Some parents expect their children to take up a career path of their choice.

Perhaps, a career that is one of the mother's or father's biggest frustrations. There are people that expect their best friends to be available for them 24/7.

Again, expectations are perfectly normal in relationships. But people should remember that others also have lives beyond a single relationship. You should not also expect another person to be responsible for your happiness. Your relationships are crucial to your happiness but how it makes you happy is completely up to you.

Communication, Communication, Communication

No relationship can ever survive without open and proper communication. This is the unifying factor in all kinds of relationships. There can be diverse personalities in a relationship yet it can still stay strong when the parties involved communicate properly. The quality of communication should be an investment in any relationship. Different people respond to different types of communication techniques, although there are general rules that apply to most relationships. In dealing with differences (which is inevitable), communication will help bring down the barriers and reach a compromise.

In order to establish open communication lines, there should be genuine interest to stay involved in each other's lives. It is a very simple but important rule. There must be a desire to relate to one another in order to encourage the other person to open up, even if there are visible differences. In a mother and son relationship, the mother must try to show the slightest interest in dinosaurs and superheroes even if she does not know anything about them. By doing this, she and her son have something to talk about.

The son will also be more open and comfortable with his mother.

Conversations are very important in a relationship. You need to engage in quality conversations to nurture the relationship. Show real interest in your conversations and always strike a balance between listening and talking. Always pay attention to the person talking and provide undivided attention as much as possible. Ask questions if you must, but be judicious in asking. Ask questions that are sensible and show your genuine interest in the topic. But before you ask questions, make sure that the person is already done talking. Many fights start because one person interrupts the other during a conversation.

Sensitivity is important in communicating with other people. Knowing what to say, what not to say, and how to say things are very important in any relationship. As other people would say, there are some things better left unsaid. There are also ways of saying sensitive things in an appropriate way.

Sensitivity and tact are things that cannot be taught completely in one sitting. It requires experience in interaction.

The best and safest way to be sensitive in your relationships is to always question your assumptions. Be transparent as much as possible and always ask questions if you need to clarify anything. If you want something, do not assume that the other person already knows what you want or what you are thinking. Not all people have psychic abilities. Maintain transparency , trust, and honesty in your relationships, especially when you get into conflicts and you have to deal with your differences.

In dealing with conflicts, do not attack the person. Instead, express how you feel with his or her actions. Attacking a person is the perfect way to build grudges and resentment, two of the most powerful weapons in destroying relationships. Focus on the problem at hand and do not drag other issues into the conversation. Be respectful at all times, taking care not to scream, curse, or raise your voice at the other person. Focus on finding a compromise or a solution instead of playing the blame-game. Finally, learn how to apologize if necessary. It is this important element that is missing in many kinds of relationships. If you have been hurt, be vocal about it appropriately. If you have hurt someone, swallow your pride and apologize.

Contributing to Another's Growth

In a meaningful relationship with anyone, it is not enough to be generous and agreeable. The best relationships flourish when two people are involved in each other's development and improvement. Therefore, you should be responsible enough to be a "police" if you see your spouse, parent, child, sibling, relative, or friend doing the wrong thing. Many people fail in this part for fear of starting a fight and ruining the relationship permanently.

Keep in mind that when you are watching out for someone else's back, it does not mean that you have to make the decision for that person. The exception would be a parent-child relationship, where children still do not have the sufficient ability to make decisions on their own. But even then, parents should already establish an environment where children can exercise their decision-making abilities and face the consequences of their decisions.

As another person in the relationship, you should only go as far as letting that person know that what he or she is doing is wrong. Express your concern but do not be judgmental. In the end, you should be able to show that person that you respect his or her final decision. Make it clear that you are only concerned and not asserting moral ascendancy over him or her.

Show that you want to help him or her by offering alternative solutions or ways of doing things.

Symbiotic Relationshi

Finally, remember that the best relationships are the ones where the give- and-take policy thrives. Accept the support from the other person and give back your support as well. Whatever relationship you are in, show kindness, understanding, and generosity. More often than not, these three elements fade away in relationships that last long because of complacency. For instance, offer to wash the dishes when your spouse just had a bad day at work. If your friend has an emergency meeting while the two of you are having coffee, offer to drive your friend if he or she does not have a ride going there. A little kindness still goes a long way in long-term relationships.

Build memories to strengthen your relationships. Make a commitment with the people important to you to spend time whenever you can. Do activities that you love doing together or try something new. Quality time will help you get to know each other better. In the process, you get to bring out the best in one another.

Nurturing any kind of relationship is hard work but it is the best investment you can make in your life. Relationships are intangible and precious proponents of happiness.

Printed by Libri Plureos GmbH in Hamburg, Germany